Shadow Standing Over Me

the Trials and Tribulations of a Ghetto Child.

Lady J

authorHOUSE®

AuthorHouse™
1663 Liberty Drive
Bloomington, IN 47403
www.authorhouse.com
Phone: 1 (800) 839-8640

Published by AuthorHouse 06/14/2017

ISBN: 978-1-5246-8977-3 (sc)
ISBN: 978-1-5246-8976-6 (e)

Acknowledgement

I would first like to give an honor to Jehovah God for without my faith I would not be alive today! My life has never been easy and I know that Jehovah see all there is to me and he knows the truth.

To my children , I just want you guys to know that even through the rough times, and we had so many. You guys made my life worth living.

From the first to the last,I have always been so thankful for the life that God gave me when he blessed me with each and everyone of you.

I LOVE YOU!

Last but not least,I would like to thank my Fiance Mr Chappell.

I want to thank you for being so understanding and your unconditional love. I thank you for believing in me and allowing me to share my life with you and not be judged. I love you!

Lady J

Chapter 1

My Life

My story began the day I entered this world. I was born in 1965 in a small city called Hamilton,Ohio (Little Chicago).

Hamilton is a place, where everyone knows your name and they will have you pronounced dead before you die.

A place where lies and rumors are believed and have destroyed so many people's lives. A place where there's never a shortage of drugs, crime and murder. A city where who and what you know can cause you to lose your life. A place where who and what you know and do can get you killed.

The daughter of two young parents in the 60's. at the time my mother was living at home with her parents. The second oldests and the oldest Girl of 17 children. Being the second oldest came with it's own set of responsibilities.

My Father was 1 of 10 children. The Only boy, living at home with his parents. Could you imagine what it was like to have 9 sisters.

After the rumors started it got back to the parents, both being concerned. The only thing left to do was talk. So now it was time for the two families to come together and talk, talk about this baby. Talk about the baby.

The first meeting took place my Mother's parents house. Standing in the dining room the question was asked. "Are you carrying our sons child? My Mother replied "NO" for whatever reason.

But because of all of the talk in the streets in

time my Grandparents took matters into their own hands. The start of Drama surrounding my life.

The next meeting was in court.

Judge Black.

At that time the parents made most of the decisions for the families. At the court hearing my mother and My father sat in the hallway as their parents went into the courtroom to talk with the judge. as the two of them sat in the hallway not really talking to each other.

Her on one side and him on the other. When the Parents came out of the courtroom, it was over. He was not the Father.

Soon after He graduated from high school he went into the military and didn't look back.

Now my mother was on her own.

with a child to raise with no father.

This created a problem for my mother and my Grandfather. he was disappointed in my mother, her being the oldest girl and a unwed mother. Home she went with her parents and things would never be the same.

IN MY GRANDFATHER'S HOUSE.

My Grandfather was a very strict man. When I look back I thought he was a mean man. Not understanding being so young. He wanted the best for his daughter. And he worked hard to provide for his family.

He worked at Fisher Body Auto plant. and in his spare time he would make things with his hands,all kinds of the things. He would work on more than one project at a time, he was very good at multitasking. When he wasn't at work at the auto body plant he was working in or around the house period he rebuilt the garage.

He would grow vegetable gardens every year. One year he grew a 12 foot tomato plant and was featured in the local newspaper.

He would make all kinds of things with his hands. Things he could sale. He would make ceramic ash trays with lighters and Fish bowls made inside the lamp. Different kind of black statues and figures. He even made me a Cherry oak Violin, we even had rabbits.

In my Grandfather's house it was rules everyone had to follow. and that meant everyone. From the tallest to the smallest.

Rule # 1. There will be no staying out all night. He felt that, if you stay out all night, that means you have another place to stay and that's where you should be. He set the all the rules in the house. Grandmother was the peacemaker in the family.

A very Beautiful soft spoken woman with a beautiful smile. A Woman of God who would hold bible studies at the house once a week.

She loved to sew, she would make clothes and tailor clothes for the people in the city.

Caring for her children was a big part of her life. Not the type of woman that went to bars or even dealt with people in the streets, unless she was working on clothes for them or passing by and speaking, everyone respected her.

By the time I turned two years old, the rules in my Grandparents became a problem for my Mother to follow. Rule # 1 was broken. Mom stayed out all night and when she return home her reality was waiting on the porch.

He had a few choice words for her and bags packed. Not only were her bags on the porch, but so were mine. He put her out and me out with her.

Grandfather, not knowing she was going to have another baby. She didn't have the heart to tell him to hurt him again.

So into the world she went.

Now to do it her way, live life by her rules.

ON HER OWN

She stayed with a friend for some time and then she got her own.

Mom got an apartment in the projects. It was a start. A A place of her own that she could afford and yes it was in the bottom,

By the time the second child was born, Mother was living her life. She had another girl, so now I have a little sister, 2 years and 2 days apart.

By the time Sister was three, Mother was spending a lot of time going out with friends. She had her own place and she now made the rules. Doing things her way and sometimes her way was not the best way.

CHAPTER 2

GOING UP THE STREET

Being young, a young mother in her first place doing things her way. Trying to find her place in this world. Taking care of home and taking care of her children, the weekend was something that she looked forward to. It was her time to go out and mix and mingle with her friends on the weekend . This night Mother had plans on going Up The Street. That's what the Grown folks would call going out at night.

Sometimes mother would have her two younger sisters babysit.

One night mother was going out and a friend was to watch Sister and I because her younger sister couldn't babysit that night.

One thing mother liked was music. she would play music all the time. at night is when she would clean the house. Burn her incense and candles and play her music.

On this particular night, she had plans on going out, so she put me and Sister in the bed and she began to get dressed to go out. Once she was dress she was waiting on the sitter. After some time, she decided to leave thinking that the babysitter was on the way. When she left, she turned all the lights off in the house and turned up radio, this way if someone came by they would think she was in the house.

Out she went, on her way up the street . As she was walking she ran into one of her friends ("Baby Sis") and they stopped and talked for a few minutes. In the conversation, Baby Sis asked Mom, "Who was watching the kids?" (Told to me by Baby Sis)and her reply was (GOD) and she went up street.

After mom left the apartment, I remember waking up to the loud sound of the radio and the darkness. The song that was playing on the radio Smokey Robinson and the Miracles *Tears of a clown* The song scared me put fear in my heart and to this day that song does something to me when I hear it.

I remember getting up to turn off the radio. I had to go into the next room to turn on a light so that I could see. I turned on the lamp and went down stairs to turn off the radio. Once I made it downstairs I remember turning the radio down a little bit and I begin to look around. I walked over to the Fishbowl it had two fish in it. A black one and a gold one. Also mom had an empty cigarette pack on the table. For some reason I opened the cigarette pack and took the black fish out of the fish bowl and put it in between cigarette pack and smashed it. To this day I don't know why I did that.

I returned upstairs and I had to turn the lamp off. when I went to turn it off, the flash caught my eye. and I flicked it a few more times. I was infatuated with the flash of the light. I turned the light switch few more times and went back to bed.

I went back to bed to only be awakened by smoke. Smoke coming from the other bedroom. As I was leaving the room after I turned off the lamp, something fell over but I never went back in the room to see what it was. It was the lamp that fell over, that started the fire.

At the time, the curtains and the lamp in the room was made out of plastic. The lamp was a fruit shaped lamp. The shade of the lamp was plastic and it melted.

When I woke up to the smoke, I remember opening the door and seeing the fire in the room across the hall. Sister was on the bed.

I tried to get sister so we could get out of the house. Sister was heavy and I couldn't carry her. I tried to and when I couldn't I pushed her under the bed and went to get help.

WE NEED HELP

Mom's aunt, "Aunt B" lived 2 rows over. Aunt B was my grandmother's sister and that's where I ran to. At the time she was home with her children watching tv.

I was told that I first came to the house and stood in the doorway and left. I returned and this time I had smoke coming off of the top of my head and I was trying to tell them something was wrong and I pointed towards the house.

At that point everyone ran out the house towards the apartment we lived in.

The smoke was so thick you could see it coming over the building.

When we made it back to the apartment the fire was coming out of the bedroom window upstairs and that's where sister was up stairs . Up stairs in the room across the hall from the fire.

Family members tried to get into the apartment to get her but the smoke was too thick. A man came out of nowhere, went into the house against the fire and the smoke and saved sister life.

I'm standing in the street looking at the fire and this was the first time I asked God for help. Help my Sister. By this time in my life my grandmother had taught me about God and how to pray.

To this day I don't know who the man was that went into the house.

After The Fire

After the fire mom had to move back home. now the relationship was strained with her father. Sister was in the hospital and my Grandmother was praying.

More and more in my Grandfather's eyes my mother was just a disappointment to him, and he would let her now.

The words he used would cut like knife.

and the expression on his face put fear in her. and he often hit her. She was afraid of him.

It got to the point that mom would sneak out to hang with her friends and would come home only to be disciplined by her father.

The last time it happened, it was time for my mother to leave her father's house. once again, this time she had two children.

Out she went into the streets. She bounced around from house to house, staying with a few of her friends. Doing everything she could at that time to hold on to us and then it became too much to handle.

A caseworker was assigned to mom's case because of the fire so that was even more pressure on her get another place of her own to prove that she was able to provide for myself and sister.

Overwhelmed Mom had to get away. Away from all that she felt was trying to stop her from living her life.

Her Father who was trying to control her life, and a Mother who was praying for her.

She had a choice to make. once her mind was made up she was going away to start a new life. But it wouldn't be that easy.

My Grandfather was not going to let her take us with her. So it came down to her going without us, Grandfather was very upset. Mom was going away. Dayton,ohio. This is when her life went from bad to worst.

Mom was gone for 3 years and Grandfather stayed mad at her. He would have his days where he would wake up in a bad mood talking about mom.

He would say things to me and at the time i was too young to understand what it meant, or even why he was saying what he was saying to me.

Every now and then Mom would call.

If Grandmother answered the phone she would let us talk to her, but if Grandfather answered he would tell her that the way she was living her life was wrong. and he never allowed us to talk to her. his way of punishing her.

One morning the mailman delivered two boxes to the house. When Grandfather read the sender's address he took the boxes out back and put them in the garage. I overheard him tell my Grandmother that the boxes was from mom and that he was going to send them back to her.

Grandmother wanted to know why. she even went as far as to tell him that it was wrong and the boxes were for the kids. He was too upset to even look at that way.

Over time when he would go to work we would go out

back and look thru the windows to try and see what was in the boxes.

One day he went to work and left the door open. I was asked by my Grandmother to go back and close the door.I took sister with me.

We walked back and looked in boxes. It was 2 giant sized stuffed animals, poodles. A pink one and a purple one. 1 for me and 1 for sister.

Over time he gave them to us and he spoke less and less about mother.

The next few years moms contact would be far and few in between.

Until one night my grandfather got a call.

It was from someone in Dayton, a stranger that was friends with my mother.

Mother was in the Hospital and she was in bad shape.

It seem the life she was living in Dayton almost took her life.

Grandfather drove to the hospital to see about his daughter.she was in bad shape almost out of her mind and she had been beaten. She was on some type of drugs and it took her some time to recover from it.

The Talk

Over time Grandfather began to be nice to her but our conversation became more serious. He would call me to come to kitchen where he would be working on a mold of Uncle's Allen's head, his youngest son. It was a Clay mold that he was working on. From time to time when Uncle Allen wasn't available for the sitting so that he could work, he would call whoever was available and this day it was my turn to sit in the chair. If he wasn't at work he was working in the garden Or he would be in his Workshop making some type of ceramic. This took time so it gave him time to think. Once he called me in the kitchen he had me sit on the chair

He started talking as if he was preparing me to leave.

He would say things like " Don't go out into the world and have babies by every Tom, Dick and Harry and not take care of them. He put emphasis on Not taking care of them. He talked to me about being in the streets. being a woman of the streets. The lack of respect and how people will talk about you and not respect you. Now at the time I was too young to understand. Too young to understand what respect meant.

The day came when mother came back. By this time she had gotten herself together and another apartment in the projects, and Sister and I was going to live with her.

Chapter 3

Vidourek Drive

1006 Vidourek Drive is the address that we moved to, across from the Little Park. We moved in I was happy I seen a lot of kids playing. A lot of kids playing by our apartment at the park. And it was a lot of people sitting on their porches. The first person that we met lived Next door. An old lady by the name of Miss Lucy and her Grandson Fred. The lady was blind but it was hard to tell by the way she would take care of herself and her grandson. She cooked and took care of her house. she would wash clothes but most of the time she sent clothes to cleaners.

Now Fred was spoiled or least that's how it looked to me. The only boy that I knew who would go to the beauty shop to have his hair done. and he dressed nice. he had everything a boy could want. The new shoes all the new games and toys.

But no Mother or Father.

When Fred would be away from the house and when she wanted him, she would call his name and after a while he would come running around the corner.

She would call his name like this, "Fred Hey Fred", Fred

Hey Fred". and sure enough he would hear her or someone in the hood heard her calling him and told him, "MISS LUCY" was calling you. And sure enough he would come running home every time.

When we first moved in we stayed in the house a lot. Mother would sleep all day and be up all night. So I spend a lot of time looking out the window

Across the walk lived a woman named Mrs.Kitty. she had husband and two sons. A light skinned one and a dark skinned one with light brown eyes. Her Husband was a big man and I never seen him smile. When he would come home, we would be at the park playing and as soon as he would go in the house we would hear him cursing. Him yelling at Mrs Kitty and doors being slammed. and that always meant it was time to go in the house.

The Summertime in the projects would be Fun and Hot. Mother had fans in the windows at night after we would get our baths we would lay under the fan and watch and listen to people walking by. Some nights you would hear music coming from down the street from someone's apartment. other nights you would hear people talking loud and cursing. It was like that in the Hood.

People would leave the doors open and unlocked all night.

It was safe like that.

Vidourek drive, was a main street in the projects on the back street of our apartment buildings .

And it was a park in front of our apartment,so when we did get to go outside we would spend most of our time in the park.

To the left of the park Mother had a friend named "Miss

D". she had one son and he spent most of time at his Aunt Anna/Big Mama's house. His aunt had 2 children around his age and all the kids from the neighborhood would play at or around her house.and she never let a child be hungry.

I think he liked being with the other kids at the other end of the projects. It was two parts of the projects.

The Old projects and the New projects, Bamboo Harris and Riverside side.We lived in Bamboo Harris.

CHAPTER 4

IN MY MOTHER'S HOUSE

In my Mother's house we spent most of our time on the inside,in our room. So much time that I would dream about going outside to play with my friends.

My mother would sleep all day and be up most of the night.and the next morning we had to be quiet until she got up. If we woke her up it would be hell to pay. To the point that she would just pick up something and hit me with it. So Sister and I would spent most of our time looking out the window and talking to each other.

We spent so much time in our room that i would make up games for us to play.

We had very few toys to play with so i would make things for us to play with.. And I loved looking in the magazines, especially the Holiday magazines. The holiday dresses and the holiday food. I would cut the the pictures of the people dressed up for the holiday and make Paper Dolls and I would cut the food out and the Christmas cookies so we could have a Tea party.

KEEP THIS ROOM CLEAN. When Mother would

find the paper that I cut she would throw it away. Mother was very strict and thorough about the house being clean.

So i had to find a place to hide it. it was a space in the closet that we used to play house in. The closet had two shelves in it so we could playhouse and store. I found a space in between the wood in the wall and i would hide the cutouts in the space and she never found them.

When Mother had good days we had good days. she let us go out and play with our friends and we could sit on the porch with her until it got late.

Mother spent a lot of time talking with her friends.

One night while sitting on the porch with mother, Miss D came over to talk to her. She was dressed up to go out for the evening.

She asked Mother what she was doing tonight and asked her to go up the street with her. Mother told her that she was staying in tonight, she told her that maybe she would go out with her the next time and to have a Good time and be careful. She said "OK GIRL" and walked up the street.

I remember watching her walk until I couldn't see her anymore. she was dressed up and had a smile on her face and I could smell her perfume after she walked away.

After some time Mother made us go to bed.the next morning when i got up Mother was outside in the back yard talking to some ladies by the clothes line.

By this time she notice that I was standing there and she made me get out of the doorway. so i went to the front door and Miss Lucy was sitting on the front porch. I stood there for minute watching Miss Lucy. she was watching the other kids playing in the park and speaking to people as they walked by.

As I'm watching her she's moving her head in the direction that the other kids was running . I said to myself, Miss Lucy can see.

Mother spent most of the day cleaning up and talking to her friends that came to the house as we played at the park.

Later that evening we sat on porch for little while then it was time for myself and sister to take a bath.

Mother got our bath ready and went back and sat on the porch. The bathroom was right at the top of the steps so I could hear mother and Miss Lucy talking. mother started crying for some reason. By the time I got out of the tub Mother was in the back yard talking to someone in a car that was parked outside. I could hear the conversation.

they were talking about Miss D.

I heard the two of them discuss that she was dead and another one friend of mothers killed her. Stabbed her with a knife and Miss D was going to have baby, the baby died too.

after I heard that i got out of the door before mother turned around and seen me standing there.

At that time the grown folks would tell the children to "Stop being noisy when grown folks talking", go in the other room.

I didn't want to get in trouble or a whooping for that matter.

By this time sister was standing in the front door looking out at the other kids in the park.

Miss Lucy was still on the porch. I told sister, Miss Lucy can see! she said to me, no she can't I'm telling MAMA. Being that we just got out of the tub we had our towels on. So I told sister, I said watch how her head move when people walk past and she speaks to them by name. Then I said to sister push me out the door and watch Miss Lucy turn her head.

I said on the count of three push me. One two, three.

When sister pushed me out the door, my towel fell and I grabbed it off the ground and ran back in the house. at this time mother was about to come in the house. she was saying goodbye to her friend. so she didn't see us at the front door.

That night it was hard for me to go to sleep. all I could think about was Miss D. I had never seen a dead person and I was really too young to understand what death was about. The next day when mother got up and got us dressed we asked to go outside, she told us "NO". She said that Miss Lucy told her I was outside naked. Once again I told sister, "Miss Lucy can see!" That had us stuck in the house for a few days.

After Miss D died, Mother seem to be very sad. all of the grown people were sad even the children that knew her. She was the first person that I knew who died. and it gave me a painful feeling as a child. Trying to understand the fact that I would not see her Beautiful Smile again,

as time went on Mother finally let us out of the house to play at the park. I missed playing with my friends.

As soon as I sat on the swing facing the house Miss Lucy came out and sat on her stool on the porch. Now she's looking at me and I'm looking at her. I was swinging back and forth and Miss Lucy, tapping her cane on the ground spitting out black stuff in the grass. Now I'm watching the Lady that everyone said was blind watch me.

We played all day. most of the summer when we were allowed to go outside.

We would play until it got dark. One evening while we

were at the park playing, here Miss Kitty's husband. Miss Kitty was just outside talking to Mother and Miss Lucy. As I was watching him as he walked in the house. A few minutes after he went in the house,Mrs Kitty went in the house. A few minutes later all of a sudden Miss Kitty came running out of the house screaming. Help me! help me! at this time Mother made us go in the house.

I ran upstairs to my room and watched from my window.

Miss Kittys mouth was bleeding and she was crying. she went into Miss Lucy's house and then the police came. The police went into Miss Kitty's house after talking to her. When they came out of the house, her husband was in handcuffs and they took him to Jail that night. I was Happy and I know Miss Kitty was too.

Her husband was mean man and I don't think that I've ever seen him smile.

The rest of the Summer was filled with Sunny days and Hot nights playing at the Little Park. the next few summers was about the same. Families moving in and families moving out. The winter was quiet. and we was in the house most of the winter. watching our friends playing outside. Even when it snowed and our friends were outside to playing in the snow. Mother would have to be in a good mood to let us go outside to play with our friends in the snow.

Over the winter time sister and I learned that Mother was going to have another baby in the Spring, and that we would be moving, down the street.

Hello Spring!!

By this time Mother was going to have another baby and we had to move, to a place more bedrooms and a New Park.

Chapter 5

924 Vidourek Drive

At the new house we had an extra bedroom and more children to play with. We also had a park in the front of our house, it was The Big park. and it had a Basketball court called "THE CAGE".

Mother knew most of the people that lived in the middle of the projects, that's where it was IN THE MIDDLE.

927, My first friend was Dottie.

Dottie was the 2nd oldest child of three

children. she had a younger brother and a older sister. she also had an Aunt and Uncle that that lived with them. Her Mother's younger siblings. Dottie Grandmother passed away giving birth so they came to live with the Oldest Sister. Dottie was named after her Grandmother.

925 is where Sue lived, she was the oldest of three, she had a younger Brother and Sister. and they both lived in the apartment behind us.

Next door on the right lived Miss Barbara, she had a daughter named Alicia. Miss Barbara was a white woman that looked like Elvis before he died. and she had a cat named Freddy.

Next door to Miss Barbara lived Miss Denmark. Miss Denmark didn't like cats at all and if you walked in her yard she would yell at you and tell you to get off the grass. Yes in the projects you were not allowed to walk on the neighbors grass. Mr.White was good for catching people walking on his grass. You wouldn't even see his face but put your foot on his grass and you would hear his voice! He would yell at you get off my grass!

Next door on left lived Miss Alice,she had two daughter's. The oldest daughter had long Beautiful hair and big Beautiful eyes. And next door to Miss Alice lived Miss Shirley. Miss Shirley had two daughters. Netta and Tinkerbell. Tinkerbell was a baby just beginning to walk.

Living in the middle was fun. it was always someone to play with and you would always see someone walking by.all kind of people.

Old, young and in between. Black,White, Mixed. Not too many White people lived in the projects, but from time to time a family would move in and try to survive. But there was one white girl a lot of the people in the projects knew. By the name of Angel, Beautiful with blonde hair and was she hip to what was going on in the streets. She was like a black woman trapped in a white woman's body and she also dated black men. And she was also a booster and she always had the nicest clothes and something to sale.

Vidourek Drive, the street itself has so many stories to tell. people from all walks of life.

Saturday mornings was always my favorite.watching the early morning cartoons, eating cereal and playing in the back with my friends.Most of the time I had to wait for mother to get up to go out. some time I would sneak out. I had to be very quiet.

It seem like my friends could go outside whenever they wanted to. or at least that's how it looked from all the days I was watching from my window.

My friend Dottie would see me in the window and she would come stand in the yard talk to me from my window or we would talk through the mail slot. But once we were able to go outside, we found something to do. Every now and then mother would send me to the store. Dick's, Dick Lawson's. was the name of the store and it was on the corner of Front and Walnut Street . So that meant I had to walk through the projects to get to the store. This would be the one time that I could look at everything as I was walking by. And my eyes were always open. Early Saturday morning you would see everything that happened late Friday night. You would see people that been out all night and we're on their way home. I would always see a wino. And his name was Dupee Clemons. Dupee would stop me and talk to me. he would tell me all the time you look just like your father! Your father is my best friend. Now at this time I didn't know who or what he was talking about. At this point I had never even seen my father not even a picture of him.

This Saturday morning I made it to the store safely. Walking past the debris left from the night before. I Always looked on the ground when I walk it seems I always found money and that morning I did. And on the way back I ran into a old man. A little old man by the name of Ralph Moss. As I was walking by he stopped me and started asking me questions. He asked me if I knew his name and then he told me what it was. Not only did he tell me what his first and last name was but he had seven extra last names after his last name. And I think 4 of those were late president's last names. He also done a little dance for me that made me laugh and I would try to do the dance with him. So once I made it back home from the store I went outside to play.

And now that we lived by the Big Park it was always someone playing at the park.

Across from the park was the maintenance office. in the same building where you paid the rent. and on the end of that building was The Head Start preschool building.

CHAPTER 6

GOING TO PAY THE RENT

Sometimes mother would send me to pay the rent which was fun to me. I liked to look at the Lady that collected the money. She wore bright colors and big earrings and a lot of perfume. Have you ever seen a lady that could chew and pop chewing,gum, smoke a cigarette and count money and ask you "HOW YA MAMA DOING" all at the same time while writing out your rent receipt. well Miss J could. and as she would give me mother's rent receipt before i walked away from the window she would say

"TELL YA MAMA I SAID HI".

Walking back to the apartment even though it was 50 feet away it seem like i was always taking a detour on the way back home. I would see one of my friends stop to talk and end up walking in the other direction, close to the apartment though. the back way which was around the back of the maintenance building.

On the way home I seen The Maintenance man, Mr Coleman. I met Mr Coleman when we moved in. he was hooking up the stove.

Mr Coleman was tall older man who had a wife. and he always carried a black lunch box. he was sitting on the concrete stoop by my house eating his lunch as I walked by.

He spoke as I walked by and I said "Hello" Mr Coleman and he offered me a sandwich. Mr. Coleman was kind like that. He was always nice to the kids. Mr.Coleman did not live in the projects. He lives in the big house on the corner of 2nd Street. The Big house that had a million lights at Christmas time.

His whole house would be covered with Christmas lights and it looks like the gingerbread house. After the first time he gave me a sandwich, it seemed as if he would look for me at lunch time give me one.

After we ate I made it home with the rent receipt. When I made it home Mother was cooking.

It was the springtime and she had the windows up to get the fresh air from outside.

I knew she was cooking when I walk up to the house, I could spell the food walking up the street. I couldn't say where the smell was coming from until I got close to the house. All day everyday someone was cooking and you could smell it all over.

The Baby

Mother was about to have the baby. Baby number 3. at this point I never seen sisters father and when it came to the new baby, I don't remember seeing the baby's father either. We all had different fathers.

Sister and I was excited about the baby.

The day came April 1st, and it was time for Mother to go the hospital. I was happy and I wanted a Little Brother.

Mother was gone for almost a week and when she came

home she had the Baby. We couldn't wait for her to get in the house.

Once Mother came in and sat down she opened the blanket so we could see the baby. It was another Girl (Little Sister).

She was a Beautiful Brown baby. her hair was coal black and it was straight. Her eyes Big and her eyelashes were long and black. and her fingers were long just like mine.

As Little Sister got a little bigger Mother let us help her with the baby, she would let me hold her and feed her but most of the time we just looked at her. Because of the new baby Mother was in a better mood. She allowed us more time to go outside to play with our friends. It was always something going on outside.

The weekends you would see all kinds of things and people.

There was a lady by the name of Miss Elma. Miss Elma, would come thru the park going to the bootleg house to sit and talk with her friends. When she would walk through the park going to the bootleg house she would be so nice to us. But coming back she would scared us to death! She would cuss all the little kids out at the park and tell us to go get our "Mammie". And the way she used the B word, you knew it was something bad!

I was at the park swinging by myself waiting on Sister to come out to swing with me. I was swinging trying to see how high I could go and as I was looking up at the sky. I would close my eyes and tilt my head back towards the sky and I guess it was the blood that I seen through my eyelids because of the brightness of the Sun. I was talking to God when I opened my eyes thought I seen a man walking on the roof of The Headstart building. he walked across to the other end and then he disappeared. I never seen him come back to the other side.

By this time sister came out side, Dottie was there and we had a race to see who could swing the highest. the boys could always swing higher and then they would jump out the swing when it was at the highest. We wanted to swing high like the boys and jump out the swing. we would have so much fun.

Once it got dark Mother made us come in the house to take a bath. after our baths we ate and watched tv and it was time to go to bed.

My room was on the back side and I could see the street from my window. across the street I could see Dottie and Sue's house.

Miss G was sitting on the porch. Miss G was Sue's Mother, and it was kids outside racing up and down the street.

I would watch Miss G most nights from the window. she would sit outside and watch her kids play. When I first met Miss G, I was afraid of her. I thought she was mean. if she caught you doing something wrong she would get on you and then take you to your mother and let her know. So that meant not only did you get in trouble from Miss G you also got in trouble from your mom when you got home.

She never allowed other kids to run in and out of her house, no playing in her house.

and when her kids ate snacks she would make them stay inside to eat them.

She would make Baked sweet potatoes cut in half. I always wanted one but was afraid to ask and it looked like it tasted good.

Looking out the window is how I would drift off to sleep.

That's how the next few years of my life went. watching everything from the window and swinging as high as I could and playing at the park with my friends.

All the fun we would have playing Tag, Hide go seek, Hopscotch, Four square, Tetherball,Chinese hopscotch and racing up and down Vidourek Drive.

It was always something to do or see in the projects.

I'd spend some afternoons and some evenings just sitting on the curb watching the people walk up and down the street. On the weekend you would see some of everything and everyone.

It was three men and they were different from the rest of the men. They dressed different, talked different and they walked different But they Loved everyone. I would watch them as they walked up the street I liked to watch them. their clothing would be be different and I liked it. And they would always say nice things to me, they would say that I was beautiful.

On the weekend when they went up the street. They would wear clothing items like mothers.

CHAPTER 7

THE MONSTER

By the time I turned 10 and

As Little sister got older Mother got a Job.

sometimes Aunt K, Aunt A would come over and babysit when they was not in school or working themselves.

At this time I wasn't not old enough to babysit.

One day a Friend of Mothers came over and started babysitting us. then he started living with us. From the first day we was left alone I didn't like him. he would say things to me that I didn't understand.

He would always be looking at me as if he was saying something to me in his head.

Everyday I would hate when Mother had to go to work. knowing we had to stay there with him. When Mother would go to work he would make me come down stairs where he was. or if Sister and I was outside at the park he would always call me in the house before Sister. After some time his words turned into touching and he would make me sit on his lap. Even when I would cry he would make me. He started touching and doing things to me and making me do things to him.

He would always say : Don't tell your Mother, if you do she going to beat you. He knew that she hit us often. Over time I found ways to stay away from him.and I would try to always keep my sisters close to me where I could always see them.

Before Mother went to work she would make us take a nap. when she would leave he would wake me up and make me come down stairs,Sister and Little sister would be asleep. On this day he was putting clothes in the washing machine when I came down stairs. The front and back door was closed and the shade were down.

Mother would open the windows to let the fresh air in the house and she would close them when she came home, everything was closed.

He made me come into the utility room where he was putting clothes in the dryer and he closed the door. Once the door was closed he backed me up against the wall he touched me and put his hand in my shorts and stuck his finger inside of me. I was scared and I started crying and he told me to be quiet and he kissed me in my mouth.

I tried to push him away from me and then he stopped. Before he open the door to the utility room to let me out, he said to me, " Don't tell your Mother or she's going to beat you".Then he made me go upstairs and take a bath. by the time that Sister and Little Sister woke up. I had went in the bathroom and took my bath. I was crying and I was hurting in my private area.By the time Mother came home from work I was sitting on the couch with my sisters. I wanted to tell Mother what he had done but I kept thinking about what he said.

Over time he would say that I was (fass).

and he would say I was doing things that I didn't do. In return I would get in trouble for things I didn't do.

When Mother would whoop me she would hit me with anything she could get her hands on. Today she would be put in jail for the way she would beat me.

Weeks went on and living in the house was getting worst. I spent as much time as I could at the park when Mother was home.

I was trying to stay out of her way and away from HIM. He was always telling Mother I was doing something so I would get in trouble.

One day I was at the park swinging waiting on Sister. I always had to wait for her to do anything. She came outside to the park and began to swing with me. Mother had just got us new shoes,Jelly shoes. I had red ones Sister had blue. Almost every Little girl in the projects had the Jelly shoes already and we finally got our pair.

As we are swinging and looking at our shoes, we began to swing higher and higher. I would close my eyes and pretend that I could swing high enough to be close to sun. I could see the brightness of the sun even with my eyes closed, The way the sun felt against my face made me feel as if I was close to God.

By this time other children had come to the park. now it's a group of us swinging and they wanted to race to see who could swing the highest and jump from the swings first.

We started swinging and the race was on. The next thing I knew Sister let go of the swing in the air and hit the ground. she never made a sound. she got up and ran in the house. A few seconds later I heard her scream so loud. I ran in the house to see what was wrong, Mother had a rag with ice to her face and she had a knot on her head the size of a lemon.

When Sister let go of the swing her feet slipped when she hit the ground made of concrete and she hit her head. It was the New Jelly shoes. at that point I started disliking the shoes because Sister got hurt. Mother had to take her to the hospital. The next few days we had to sit on the porch.

Sitting on the front porch was like watching tv. It was always something going. on this day Miss Alice,the next door neighbor was in the house fussing at her daughter. Our front doors are very close and her front door was open so I could hear her. Her daughter Annette was crying and asking her "Why Not" and then the door slammed.I could still hear them after the doors closed. by this time Mother made us come in the house. I had to use the bathroom so I went upstairs. While in the bathroom I could hear Miss Alice and Annette thru the walls. it sound like Annette was being hit and she was screaming. The next evening I was sitting on the porch and Annette came outside and sat on the porch. at first she didn't say anything and I said hi and she spoke back. I told her, I like your hair.

Her hair was Beautiful. it was Long black and thick, it was what Black people call "Good Hair". My hair being short and nappy from that point I wanted long hair like hers. Annette was Senior in High school and she had a boyfriend that was in the Military.

She loved him and wanted to be with him and her Mother was against it. and that's what the screaming was all about. She told me she was going away after she Graduated from High School. we sat on the porch for the rest of the evening. Her talking about her boyfriend and having her own house,and me braiding her hair.

CHAPTER 8

SATURDAY MORNING

After Sister's knot went down and she was better Mother let us go back to the park

Saturday morning was my favorite day of the week.I would get up early to watch my favorite cartoons and eat cereal. this morning I heard my friends outside talking in the back. I looked out the window and seen Dottie outside so after I ate, I went outside to play.This morning we played in the back for a while and then we walked over to the Headstart building. when we walked on the side of the building it was two men sitting up against the wall of the building it looked they were dead or sleep. so we were quiet when we walked over. I picked up a rock just in case they tried to get us.and it was someone that we knew. Two men from the neighborhood that everyone knows, had been sitting on the side of the building the night before sniffing glue.both had a hard wonder bread bag stuck to their hand and dried glue around their mouth. we stood there looking at them for a minute and then I threw the rock and we ran. By this time the other kids came out to play at the park. it was always something to do in the projects. In the morning we would play at the park and at night we would play in the back of the house. In the back is where the driveway was and we could play kickball and race each other up and down the street. and the street was wide and long enough to draw a chinese hopscotch. when we played "Hide go seek" it was a Big tree in the yard at the end of the row. That night we played until it got dark and it was time to go in for baths. it seemed like the other children could always stay out longer than we could. we always had to go in first and we had days when we couldn't go outside at all.

Mother worked early in the morning so that may have been the reason.

CHAPTER 9

THE DAY MY LIFE CHANGED

The day started like every other day. Mother was getting ready for work. she had already set our clothes out for the day. And she was cooking bacon. I was sitting at the kitchen table when that man walked in the back door. He spoke to Mother and then he looked at me, so I got up and went up stairs where my sister's were. At that point I wanted to tell Mother what he had done to me but I was afraid. he already had Mother thinking I was doing things and made me get in trouble for no reason. I didn't tell her.

Mother went to work and once again I was stuck in the house with the Monster. I tried my best to stay out of his way so I stayed close to my sister's and we spent most of the morning at the park or sitting on the porch with Little Sister. after eating lunch it was time to take a nap so I got my sisters and we went upstairs to take nap. Sister liked to talk. and nap time and bedtime is when she would talk the most. Once we all were asleep the Monster came in the room and woke me up. He made me help carry some clothes down stairs. When I got down stairs he made bring the clothes in the utility room. Once in he closed the door like before. He told me to put the clothes down and take off my shorts. I told him no and he said that i better or he would make sure I got beat when Mother came home. I told him no again and that's when he pulled them down himself.

He made me lay down and he began to put his mouth on my private part sticking his tongue and finger inside of me. I tried to stop him and wanted to scream he was hurting me but he put his hand over my mouth and he tried put himself inside of me. At that point I somehow in my mind,Blacked out, to another person in another place.This would be the first time that I blacked out, as he raped me. before it ended, He told me this is what all men wanted from me and that I better not tell. He said this to a Ten year old child.

When it was over he ran water in the tube and made me take a bath and go back to take a nap. I cried while I was in the tub and I didn't want to wake my sisters I wanted Mother to come home. After our nap we sat on the porch. Sister played at the park while I sat with Little Sister.I did everything I could not to go in the house where the Monster was. I sat there on the porch until Mother came home. When the time came I could see Mother by the cage which is the Basketball court and I wanted to get up and run to her and tell her what happened. I sat there and as she walked up she looked at me and asked me "What's wrong" I said nothing. sitting there thinking about what he done and what he said. I didn't want to get in trouble.but soon after I did tell. Mother was upset, and she was even upset with me as if I did something wrong and I got a whoopin. and when it all came out the only thing Mother could do was expose the Monster. Mother upset and hurt because she trusted him. she wanted to hurt him as well and my Grandfather and a few other men that was friends with Mother. The Monster is gone!

CHAPTER 10

WHEN PEOPLE FOUND OUT

When everything came out and people found out about what happened I was being treated different. It seemed like for a little while I couldn't play with my friends.

And They weren't allowed to play with me. Except for Dottie. And I notice when people looked at me they would whisper or say things under their breath as I walked by. After some time went by things was almost normal, normal as can be.I was standing on the porch when Mother had me come in the house because she wanted to talk to me. she wanted to talk to me about going to camp.Camp Campbell Guard. at this time I didn't want to be away from her. I told her I didn't want to go.She already had it arranged. I'm pretty sure the social worker set it up. And sister and I was to go to camp later that month. When the day came it was raining. I even at that point wanted to stay at home with Mother. Sister and I had to go. Mothers friend "Mr Q" was driving us to the camp.As we were driving away from the complex I felt as if Mother was going to drop me and not come back and I cried for a minute as I looked back at the projects. This would be my 1st time being away from the children that I play with everyday and Mother. As we drove down the wet road I kept looking back. I wanted to go back home. Then all of sudden the car went off the road and down a hill and crashed into a tree. Sister and I were in the back seat and the seat lifted up on one side and we slid to the other side from the impact of the crash. Mother was crying and she said that her foot was hurting. Mr Q was ok and he went to get help. Mother went to the hospital and we still had to go camp.

The first night it was hard to sleep being away from Mother. all I could think about was her being hurt and how much I wanted to go home the first night was rough.The next morning we got up for breakfast. all the girl at the camp ate together and the girls that slept in my cabin ate together at the same table.We had to pass the different dishes to each other and say "Please" and "Thank you" while doing it. That was my first time I experienced that, something that we didn't do at home. It was also my first time that I spent the night with a white girl. The only time I had ever been around white people was at the Welfare office, Doctor's, School or at the Grocery store when Mother would let us go.Not many white people lived in the project's at that time. Overall it was a good experience I made new friends but I still missed Mother. The day came and it was time to go home and I was ready and happy.The trip to camp was arranged to take my mind off of what the Monster done to me. And when it was time to go home, I was sad that I was going home. I made New friends and learned some new things.

When it came time to go home,all the girl met up by the buses to be picked up. I noticed that it was only a few black girls and the majority of the girls being picked up we're being picked up by their mother and father.

When Mother came I was so Happy to see her.

CHAPTER 11

BACK HOME

I'm back home now and I missed Mother and Baby sister so much.I sat on the porch holding Baby sister for a while. we sat and watched the other children play at the park. I wanted to play kickball but the City workers was pouring blacktop on the street behind the house and it was dangerous for us to play so we had to stay in front. As I was sitting on the porch and my neighbor Netta came outside with her Little sister Tinker. so we walked the babies around the block.

We walked to back of the house just to look and then we went back to the park. by this time Mother called me in to eat. After we ate it was time to take a nap . I could hear the men working on the street and children playing as I was going to sleep. when I woke up I went down stairs Mother was standing in the back talking and once again I was standing in the door looking out.

I could see the Ambulance from the door.When Mother came in she said that somehow Netta slipped into the hot tar that was being poured on the street and she was burned really bad. and for the next few days we couldn't go in the back of the house we could only play at the park.Over the next few years I started noticing a lot of things. A lot of things that a child shouldn't have to worry about or even think about for that matter.My Life changed and I became aware of different situations around me. I spend a lot of time sitting on the curb thinking. And waiting for somebody to come and play with me. I had a friend named Michelle. Michelle was a few years younger than me. Michelle was also deaf and she couldn't speak. but I could understand her and she could understand me. Then we had a new family that moved in and they also had a daughter that was deaf and couldn't speak,but she could say f*** you.Her name was Alice. By the time the fall set in it was time to go to school. I liked to going to school, I also loved my first grade teacher Mrs Reed. By the time I was in the 5th grade my mother's life had went through one extreme to the next. That's when I experienced my first shootout. Mother had a new friend named "DT". And one afternoon he ran in the house and told all of us to get down on the floor. I could hear the gunshots. He and another man "L,H" got into a fight about Mother. He wasn't around for long. After the shootout we spent the majority of our time in the house. Me looking out the window and looking at the highway. You could see the highway from my bedroom window. I would just watch the cars go by. Wondering where all the people was going. With so much going on I was glad to see winter coming.People tend not to do as much in the winter time outside,One night that winter we had a snow storm. So I sat up most of the night listening to wmoh radio station to see if we had school the next morning. The snow was coming down real heavy and it was real quiet outside. As I'm looking out the window

I thought I seen something move across the highway. Then I thought it was my imagination because I had a way of imagining things in my mind. And then I seen it again So I woke sister up to tell her to look. and at that time I seen two Objects move across the highway it actually looks like two little snowmen. After a few minutes of watching out the window I went downstairs and told mother that I seen something moving on the highway. And I had her come to the window. Once she came to the window she seen it also. So we put our coats on and we went over to the highway. it was a big fence before you could get to the highway. So I climbed over the fence and it was two white dogs, Big white dogs. They were trying to cross the street. As I got up onto the highway,I called the dog that was closest to me. At the same time the other dog was trying to cross the street and it was hit by a car. The dog that I had in my hand was crying I never knew that a dog could cry. So I got the dog and carried it down to the fence and handed it over to mother. We took the dog in the house and got it warm, the dog had a dog tag on it. So Mother called the number on the tag and the police also. We had the dog for a few days. It played with me but you could tell it was sad. Then the owner came to pick the dog up. It was a White lady. When the lady came to the door and Knocked, I think the dog knew it was her. Because it started barking but it was barking as if it was calling out to her. Once we open the door the dog ran to the lady and she was crying. She said that the dogs got out somehow and she had been looking for the dogs for 3 days. And that they were sisters, once she put the dog in the car, I took her and showed her where the other dog was. She had someone coming to pick it up she said that she would bury the dog.

I will never forget that day for the rest of my life. It was the first time I thought my mind was playing tricks on me. The winter came and went, spring came and went. Once again it's the summertime and I'm beginning to babysit. I had a few babysitting jobs. Mother and her single girlfriends. Looking back I may have kept 55% of the kids in the projects. I had one couple that I babysit for and they had one son that they called Boo Boo. Marla and Prince. When I would baby-sit it would be in the evening before they went out. So BooBoo would already be fed and ready for bed. we would watch TV until we fell asleep. One night while I was sitting out on the curb by the tree. It seemed as if it was always something bad happening. Or maybe things was always happening and I was just too young to understand. I became more aware of my surroundings and the pain where I lived. The pain from the people, other people's pain. Between babysitting and playing with my friends when I could, it was always something. And it always happened on the weekend, always. One weekend in July my three friends went out. The 3 men that dressed different. And when they would go up the street at night they would be dressed as women remember I said they were different than the other men. However while they were out, one of them was picked up by a white man. He picked him up to go on a date. In other words, Trick with her. Not knowing it was a man. And it may have been more than one man in the van. but they took him to Peck Boulevard to engage in a sexual act, with what they thought was a woman. When they found out it was a man they beat him and hung him in a tree and killed him. They also and cut his penis off and put it in his mouth. I may have been a child, but I'll never forget that for the rest of my life because they had his funeral around the time of my birthday if not on my birthday that year in July. From that point on I have never liked garlic Franks.

More and more I started to notice how things changing around the neighborhood. and for myself I had a lot going on in this little head of mine I often payed attention to everything that was going on around me. I began to be more concerned about adult matters I begin to worry about things as if I was grown. Over the next few years it was so much going on that I had to find a way in my mind to escape the madness. so it seemed like every time something would happen I could make myself pretty much disappear from the scene.I would always make myself someone famous. Imagine that I was somewhere else living another life. In my life things begin to change as I began to get older.The summer came and went. And it's time for school.All of the children in my row went to the same school.So every morning the kids in my row would meet up and walk to school together. On this morning I was late for school. And I walked across the street and knocked on the doors of my friends to have someone to walk with. Everyone was gone already. I was late So i went on to school. At lunchtime I was sent to the office to get the lunch tickets and I seen Sue and her brother and sister leaving. When I got home from school that day Mother told me that MissG had died. She committed suicide something that I didn't understand as a child. After some time it seemed as if everyone began to move. I missed my old friends. one family moved to California and the other family move to Middletown And we moved to the other end of the projects. Making new friends was always the hardest. And at this time I was old enough to babysit so I spent the majority of my time babysitting for all of my mother's friends when they went out on the weekend. This is when I started learning about the street life.

CHAPTER 12

STREET LIFE

I was the babysitter for the majority of the major players in the game in the City of Hamilton in the bottom at that time. From my babysitting experience I *seen* everything from physical abuse, drug abuse even death. I also seen what I thought was love. I realized then that men had a way of doing things. And the women often suffered from having a broken heart and would suffer behind the way they would Compensate for the pain. It seem like there were a lot of families where there were a lot of children and single Mothers . Only a few of my friends had their fathers living under the same roof. And I mean a few. A few of the women had relationships with men most times unhealthy.

Marla had a husband named Prince. he was a very quiet man.My grandmother would tailor suits for him. And he would dress up with the wide brim hats and step out with his friends. I seen another side of him. he would be very abusive to Marla. One night Prince and his friend went up the street and the later that night Prince and his friend was driving on Peck Boulevard and had a bad accident. The car he was riding in wrapped around a tree or it was split in half either way it killed him instantly. after Prince's funeral Marla moved away and I never seen her or boo boo again from that day to this day. I had another couple that I babysat for and they had two children. A boy and a girl and the Father was Major Player in the game.I could tell by the way people would greet him.also the House that they lived in was really nice. Big screen tv's in the 70's. Top of the line cars.I got paid good for babysitting.I also watched his Brother's kids. They had two daughter's. He was also in the Game. He drove a two toned Lincoln continental with sliding doors you have to remember this was in the late seventies early eighties. That was just A few of my first babysitting jobs.

CHAPTER 13

MOVING AGAIN
WALNUT DR,

We moved from the back of the project where we couldn't see anything except the people that lived around us and the highway to being right smack dab in the Front of everything. Front Street was the main street and as soon as you walked out of our house you're are on Front Street. I knew a lot of the people that lived on this end of projects. some of the kids would come to the other end and play in the summertime. Now I'm a little older my sisters have gotten older and I was definitely changing. Mother's life is changing as well, she had a boyfriend. From the time I seen his face, I was confused about why he was there.He would only come on the weekends.and the most he ever stayed was the weekend. Over time he brung a little boy with him, come to find out it was his son. for a while things were going good for mother and her new friend. when he would come around mother would be so happy. and I could always tell when things are going bad. she would be very moody and mean most of the time and she would slept a lot. By this time in my life I had learned her ways so I would do everything I could to stay out of her way. And try to keep her happy because if not the abuse would start. The mind games.Sometimes she would get upset or she would be mad about a boyfriend and I would be the one she would take it out on. Not saying that I was an angel or a saint I'm pretty sure I done things but not to deserve the abuse she gave me. I was forever blocking her from hitting me with a stick or something and she was forever hitting me in my head or my arms with a stick. so I would often have to defend myself. I learned a way and learned how to protect myself by staying out of her way. Also our housework would double. we would have to clean from the time we got up until it was dark. and then maybe we could go outside if it was still early enough. at least once or twice a month my mother would get on her hands and knees and hand wax the floors.

and when she was waxing the floors me and my sisters would be washing the walls and the baseboards.Mother always made sure we had a Beautiful clean home to live in. she was very creative when it came to decorating the house. She would take nothing and make something. and she love plants we had plants everywhere in living room. She would actually take Miracle Whip and rub each leaf of the plant for nourishment. After our work was done we were allowed to go outside. I made a few new friends and I had some old friends from the other end of the projects. My first friend was a boy his name was Robert. Robert Gates. "Birmingham" is what his friends called him. His family was his was originally from Birmingham Alabama. we also attended the same junior high school. Roosevelt Junior High. Roberts mother work at the dry cleaner and I think he may have been the only boy that I knew whose clothes were dry cleaned in Jr high beside Fred, at that time. People was washing their clothes and hanging them on the clothesline. Or drying them in the house if you had a clothes dryer we did. And we ironed them ourselves. Robert was kind of spoiled he was the youngest of two children he had an older sister. His sister was a Jack of all trades .When I say she could do some hair. she would carry her cutting shears in her purse because people would stop her on the street and ask for a haircut. but her real gift was singing. The first time I had ever heard her sing was at a talent show. At the Booker T Washington Community Center. the talent shows was something that would come once a year and we would be so excited about going.Everyone with Talent would perform in the show.Hamilton's version of Showtime at the Apollo.Hamilton had it's own Stars. The Hometown of Roger Troutman and The Zapp band, it started here.Lee James was our James Brown. I would watch his sister sing, and she would just take me to another world.

With her gift from God. My other Friend was a Girl. Karhonda. Between babysitting for my mother and babysitting for her friends the other little time I had I spent with my new best friend. We did all kind of things together fun things mostly ate.

It seems her mother was always cooking something and she made the best chicken and rice I've ever had. We would spend a lot of time walking around and talking. Talking about boys. Karhonda played in the marching band at school. We would talk and laugh about everything. My Best Friend. We would take a walk at least three nights a week. 6 p.m. we would take a walk and our routine was the same every time. We walk up walnut to 2nd street which is where the square is. It's now called Baily square. back in the day that's where everyone hung out in the summertime. Cars Parked people standing outside smoking a joint drinking a beer, drinking some wine just talking. Anyone that you wanted to see would be on the Square in the evening. Then we would walk down 2nd Street towards Hanover by the Catholic Church. People would sit on the Catholic church steps and just talk. It never failed when we would walk past the Phone Booth, that was on the corner of 2nd Street the phone would ring. For some reason the phone with always ring when we walk by most of the time. It was a boy pretending to be crying saying that he was looking for his mother and she left with a black man. Someone playing a joke we would tell him to call the police! And then it was back to the house a lot of times once it got dark we couldn't go out of the projects so we was behind Front Street line.

One night it was a lot of traffic on Front Street I went to the window to see what it was. It was a lot of police cars out on front street and I could hear my mother saying to Robert, stop throwing rocks at the police cars and go home. something happened and it was some kind of riot with police. a few people were arrested and hurt. A few days later I was sitting on the front porch something I did from time to time. Robert came by and he stopped and talked to me. I asked him why was he out there throwing rocks at the police. Robert was kind of a bad boy. He rode his bike everywhere riding on the curbs jumping the curbs and popping wheelies in the middle of the street. a lot of girls liked Robert. to the point where a few girls had a fight over him. these girls didn't live in the projects. so in the evening we had to be close to the house. I could go around to his house and he was also welcome at mines. and we would talk about everything talk about all the girls and I didn't realize at the time that he had a crush on me. Or should I say he liked me. he would ride up on me on his bike and scared me.He would always say something sweet or funny to me. I can say this was the first boy that I had a crush on. first boy that made me smile. one day Robert's mother was at work and he asked me to come over. so I went over to talk to him. he asked me to come upstairs in his room he was hanging up some clothes. We sat in his room for a little while talking and this is when I had my 1st kiss. he asked me if he could kiss me and I wanted to kiss him too and we did.After that kiss every time I would see him I would have this funny feeling on the inside. it was a feeling that almost made me sick but in a good way. He was just my friend. It would be days that I would be sitting in front of the house and I would watch the girls that liked Robert go and visit him. You have to walk by my house to get to his house. and when they would leave he would walk them up the street but he always stopped and talk to me. Even with the girls with him,he would stop and talk to me. Robert was kind of mature for his age and he hung around older guys. mainly the hustlers in neighborhood. and he would go to places that grown people went to. one night Robert and his friend Tracy Barlow went to a bar called Ben's in New Miami. and something bad happened that night. all I know is that Robert and Tracy were involved in a bad accident that took both of their lives Robert died instantly. from what I was told he was split straight up the middle from the accident and Tracy lived a couple of weeks and then he died. It was so many stories going around and I don't think we'll ever know the truth of what happened to them that night. now the atmosphere in the project was sad and gloomy so many people loved him.

it was a lot to take in and to see his mother walk around wearing his tan jacket that he wore all the time was really sad. He was her everything. All I could do was tell Miss Bernice was that I loved her and if it was anything I could do for her all she had to do was ask. His funeral is one of the saddest things I've experienced. To see his mother cry and his sister, his friends and this is when I realized how many girls really liked Robert. The ones that thought they were his girlfriends and then me his Friend Girl.

CHAPTER 14

MOTHER

Soon after that it seems that mother started having problems in her relationship. And she and I began to get into it more and more. For one reason or another. Sometimes I felt like she hated me. After dating this man 5 to 6 months She found out that he was a married man with a son.

He started coming around less and less. It went from every weekend to every other weekend to once a month.

This particular weekend was different. mother had clean the house and prepared to see him. it was just a little things that she would do for herself as a woman to prepare for a man. Most of the time I felt like she cared about the men more than she cared about myself and my sisters. It was the special way she cared for them, The way she took care of them.

Even when it came to her preparing a meal for the men that she dated. They would have steak and myself and my sisters would have Bologna. I always knew when he was coming.and those would be the days that my mother would be the happiest. And the other two to three weeks was almost like hell.

This particular weekend when he visited it was on a Saturday. And it was late in the evening about 9 o'clock . And at this time it was time for my sisters to go to bed and would go in my room and watch TV . So we went upstairs and then later on they came upstairs and went into mother's room and I heard her door shut. my bedroom was across the hall from the bathroom which was really like being across the hall from her bedroom. I could hear them talking and having sex, even though I tried to go to sleep. After some time I heard mother crying and I heard him say a few words. I could hear his footsteps in the hallway. once he began to walk down the stairs I heard a pop. I set up in my bed because the sound scared me and I didn't know what it was. I also heard him stop a on the stairs and continue down the stairs after the Pop. I heard the door open and close. So I got up and went in the hallway I could see mother's door was open and I could see her laying on the bed so I walked in her room and walked over to her. she had a gun in her hand and Blood on her gown, she shot herself. I called her name a shook her.When I tried to help her, she looked up at me and pushed me away, I think she wanted it to be him that came back and help her.

But it was me. And he walked out on her even after he heard the gun go off. so she got up and she was crying and she was saying something that I didn't understand and she was dressed in a white sheer nightgown and it had blood on it. I couldn't tell where the blood was coming from but it was a lot of blood . she began to walk in the hallway stumbling and she went downstairs. I followed behind her. she looked out the door and she didn't see him and it made her cry even more. it was late outside but no one was really out. and next thing I know I was following her as she walked towards the sand park. And on the other side of the highway is the great Miami River. It was maybe a block-and-a-half from where we lived . as we were walking through the park I began to plead with her. I was telling her that everything was going to be ok. and that you don't need that man. and as I'm telling her this, we're getting closer to the Bridge,the river and we're about to cross the highway. Once we cross over the highway she began to climb up on the side of the Bridge. I begged and I pleaded and I told her how much we loved her and how much we needed her and that she needs to come home with me.

Mother's heart was broken once again. She was crying so hard that when she tried to talk it didn't make sense to me. As I pulled on her gown crying and asking her to please come with me she began to let go….

About the Author

Feel that my life experiences qualifies as a reason for me to write the book. The different situations that I have overcome in my life.

I realized a few things about life at an early age The Good The Bad and The Ugly. I seen it I lived it and I overcome so many obstacles from the life.

I am the oldest of five children. Born and raised in Hamilton Ohio. Second ward the bottom is what it's called. It seems that I could stand on every street corner and give you a story about the history of my city. Growing up in the second ward being from the streets and experiencing and surviving so much. So much that if I was standing on a sidewalk beginning as a child with all my friends and we walk up the street. As we continue to walk my friends disappear simply because of the experiences in life. Being incarceration death or drugs. Yes there are success stories but you can't hear about them or share within if they don't come around. Meaning the people.

Printed in the United States
By Bookmasters